JENNIFER LOVES TO WORK AT HOME

Guidance on Finding Work at Home Employment

JENNIFER LOVES TO WORK AT HOME
jennifer_gaillard@yahoo.com

I would like to thank my husband Jerome for his continued support and motivation. A special thank you to my children.   To the person motivates me daily, my friend Kimberly, thank you to the moon and back!

Jennifer Loves to Work at Home

Jennifer Loves To Work at Home

Guidance on Finding Work at Home Employment

Thank you for investing in you!

As you may know already, my name is Jennifer Gaillard and I want to welcome you to Work At Home experience. I know that the idea of working at home may seem far-fetched and or too good to be true but I am here to tell you that it is possible. I am going to work with you and mentor you into success.

A little about me:

I started working from home in 2009. I was a single mother with 3 small children. We were cooped up in a single wide mobile home, where I had to train them to respect my job, so that I could provide for my family. Time, my small children learned how to watch television respectfully, keep out of my bed room when Mommy worked and write me a note when they wanted a snack or had an altercation. I had my cousin come in a baby sit for me, when I needed to work long hours during the day time. I wanted to share that little bit about myself because I know you may want to learn, how to manage working from home, with a family. It is attainable and manageable. The key to success is **communication, persistence, and consistency**!

Objective:

Provide important details that you will need as you apply for work at home jobs. These are some of the notes that I've taken and skills that I have learned to help me land just about any job that I have applied for.

You've made an excellent decision. I want to share all that I know with you. These are some of the most common attributes employers are looking for, during the application and hiring process:

Popular Skills Work at Home Employers Look For During an Application:

1. Effective Communication Skills (written and oral)
2. Great listening skills
3. Knowledgeable
4. Organized
5. Time Management
6. Professional
7. Goal Oriented
8. Willingness to learn
9. Able to efficiently and effectively solve problems
10. Experience
11. Able to build relationships

How it works:

- Working at home is simple. Different employers provide different services. Some employers provide equipment (computer, phones, pay your internet and phone bill etc.), while others require that you have your own computer.
- There are hourly jobs, jobs where you choose your own shifts (flexible), and contractual jobs.
- Work at home employers are the same as working at a physical office. You have to be there on time and ready to work. You may get hired for a full time, part time, or seasonal position.

Your responsibilities:

- Have high speed internet (at all mean necessary. If you have to temporary go to a friend's house that has high speed internet, go there! You have to do what you have to do to get your feet in the door)
- Make sure you have a working LAND LINE phone. Try not to give anyone that number and request that the provider give you the least amount of features possible. I have only basic calling service, no caller ID, call waiting, or anything! This is my dedicated work line.
- Be at work on time. Have your family up to par!! Let them know that this is your job! Everyone has to be on one accord and that includes family and friends that may want to visit. Make sure they understand, you work from home and they cannot just pop up and visit you when they want. Make sure your background is as noise free as possible.
- Have a dedicated work space. Grab you a nice plant from Walmart, by you a $30/$40 fax machine / printer (not required but a great time saver!) Decorate your office, or bed room (my office is in my laundry room) and make your money!
- Employers are going to want a lot of paper work from you, if you don't have the funds to get a fax machine, no worries. If you have a smart phone, you can have the forms emailed to your email address. Download this application via your Apple Store or Google Play Store account or visit the website and create you an account https://www.docusign.com , you can sign all the paperwork without having to print the papers out. Go to http://faxzero.com/ and fax the paper from your mobile device/ computer. This saves me a TON of time.

Let's get to work!

Here are some of the employers that I have worked with. These are legitimate employers that I want you to start with.

1. http://www.sykes.com/
2. http://www.westathome.com/
3. http://www.convergys.com/
4. https://www.sedgwick.com/
5. http://conceroresources.com/ (This is a certified staffing agency. Scroll and search for work at jobs on this page)

Your success starts now. These are only a few of the many legitimate work at home opportunities. I recommend creating a profile on all of the websites. Type in work at home jobs and start applying.

1. http://www.indeed.com/
2. http://www.monster.com/
3. http://www.careerbuilder.com/

These are not the only legitimate work at home jobs available. Search for more jobs, and keep applying. Where you currently are in your life, does not dictate where your future will be. Stay motivated and encouraged. I'm here to make sure you are successful. It's not just the money, I want to help.

Steps to getting hired:

1. **Put in applications!** If you don't apply for jobs, then you are not applying yourself! Make applying for a job, a part of your schedule. The job you land may not be the highest income that you've ever made, but the goal is to get hired, get experienced and update your resume with these magical words...
<mark>I HAVE WORK AT HOME EXPERIENCE</mark>!

2. **Make sure your resume skills and catches the employer's attention.** Did you take time to review your resume to make sure it is free of grammatical errors? Did you include too little information or too much information? You don't want to have too much information on a resume. Make sure your contact information is accurate. Make corrections and personalize your cover letter and resume to reflect the job that you are applying for.

3. **Tests:** Yes, some jobs will test your reading, writing, mathematical, and typing abilities. Make sure you have a calculator handy along with a paper and pen. Have your phone beside you, in case you need to google some information. (some jobs will have you define words) If typing is your weakness, practice, practice, practice! I've included a link that increased my typing skills
http://www.typingtest.com/

4. **Check your email!**!! This is very important. The majority of employers will contact you by email versus telephone. It's the new preferred contact method and it's convenient. Make sure your email has a presentable name that will not cause an employer to pre judge you.

5. **Acing the interview!** How I love interviews. This is your time to shine! Have a plan. Research the company, take notes, have a love one interview you and leave a lasting impression! Don't let the interview make you nervous, show the interview why you are a professional! It's your job, go get it!

6. **Follow up with a thank you email.** Ask the interviewer for their email address. Surprise them, send them a friendly, professional email. Thank them☺

7. **If the employer takes too long to respond, YOU CONTACT THEM!** Like I said in step 5, it's YOUR job, go get it!

What's going on in your background?

Work at home jobs are just like working in a call center. You need to have a made up mind that you are coming to a real job, every day.

The employers pay great detail to your background noise. Take the dogs outside, or in a room far away from you. Make sure there are no babies crying or fighting teens in the background!

These are definitely a "no, no"!

Are you listening?

Did you properly read the question during the application? Are you taking notes? Listening skills are vital in having a successful career.

Networking

Create a network base. There are lots of people that do what I do. They work from home. When you work from home, you need to have a positive team of people around you. Search online, connect with coworkers, and browse Face Book. Find people that will help you get on the career path that you desire. When you get hired, find coworkers and add them as friends on your Social Network Page.

Use your resources

My handy tool is internet! How sweet it is. The internet is the gateway to us landing any job we want. You have access to the highest paying jobs online. Research, follow up with you jobs, go on YouTube and watch videos. These tools are readily available for you all the time. Use them. I watch videos online and I learned a great deal. I will include some websites where people, just like you and I have found legitimate jobs and can help you start making big bucks in little of no time. I know the entire application process can see overwhelming but your test, will become your testimony.

https://www.youtube.com/watch?v=9OaU7ZquJi0
https://www.youtube.com/watch?v=1PeGUMkR8Ec

You've have already made the first step into making this official and you have the tools and the knowledge to become successful. You have the drive and ambition to reach your career goals. You have to believe in yourself, step outside of the box, and put in effort to get hired. If you lack getting a response from your application, then it's time to get an upgraded resume. It's time to fly, and make this dream a reality!

Much love and success,

Jennifer G.

Jennifer Loves to Work at Home

Contact information

Jennifer Gaillard

Email Address: jennifer_gaillard@yahoo.com

Jennifer Loves to Work at Home

Jennifer Loves to Work at Home

Jennifer Loves to Work at Home

www.ingramcontent.com/pod-product-compliance
Lightning Source LLC
Chambersburg PA
CBHW041133200526
45172CB00018B/367